Environment

The concept of compatibility

for continuous results

Joba Adekanmi

Environment

ISBN 978-1-914528-09-5

Published in United Kingdom by:
Impact Publishing House

www.TheServantandKing.com
iph@TheServantandKing.com

Contents

Preface

Some things happen around you consistently in certain places with limited human intervention. You can observe the changes after leaving them or see activity and organised transformation after the last human intervention. It is a crucial concept that helps automation or the idea of allowing things to run themselves even when no one is there.

A farmer plants a bean seed, and it grows from the soil. A lioness delivers a cub in the grassland, and the baby lion grows to maturity. Cows produce calves that mature to become dolphins in the ocean. A fish gives birth to a fry in water, which develops into fish.

Fish is born in water. They grow, mature, and produce offspring, continually growing and surviving in the same place.

Seeds grow in the soil and can maximise their potential to bear fruit or become a tree. However, that is only the case sometimes, only when you can find the right match of conditions for the seed. Some places make it impossible to experience any change, let alone germinate or grow, while others may help it start the growth process but never allow it to reach its full potential.

There is a place meant for the seed and everything; that place is where it can function not just for a while but to its full potential, and that place is called the habitat or environment. It is where they are comfortable, can relate easily, function with other parts, and maximise their full growth potential. So the environment where anything can thrive or succeed is based on its characteristics.

It is a fundamental concept of success. Your habitat is where your characteristics are recognised. You can easily find nourishment and support in a chain of events designed to help all parties involved mutually exist and benefit. Many places can accommodate you, but only a few can transform you. Some may tolerate or abuse your potential, but there is an environment that will unleash it.

There are so many things we see around us. They are in their place. Scientists have done so much work over the years to search and research, discovering new things in diverse places, but they also take note of the area and the environment because it is essential. Experiments have shown the relevance of the habitat to the things we see in nature. Living things underdevelop or die because they cannot function or thrive in a different place outside their habitat, which points to the critical role it plays in their growth and development. It is essential, not just anywhere, but in the right place, as there is a place for everything.

If you want to make things also, you must recognise the importance of the environment in its success, or else you will have gone so far but return to learn the lesson that nature teaches us.

I am confident that you made the right choice by picking this book. 'Environment' would have achieved its aim when it exposes the truth and shines the light for you to see. It will help you understand one factor that could make you thrive, a significant one worthy of consideration in producing products that can keep yielding even after your last action.

Introduction

Have you ever thought of the things you have to do daily and how many of them you have to do, again and again, the same way?

Everyone does something, and many people will have to do the same thing again sometime afterwards. It could be minutes after, hours after, days after, weeks after or even years after the previous action. It could be any activity relating to you, your work, the services you provide to other people or what you produce. Consider it carefully; is it the same input and activities every time, with the same and corresponding output on every occasion? Do you have to go through the same process every time you want to produce that same result? I wonder what your answers would be.

Imagine you invested so much effort and time to complete a task or series of actions, and you were so pleased by the results you achieved. You had a feeling of completion and a sense of accomplishment. It does not usually stop there. You now want to make it happen again. What would you do? Start all over, doing what you have once done. Yes, again. How does that sound?

I believe you must have done something that brought you your desired expectation. You completed it with joy at the first instance, but now you have to go through the same process to keep getting that same result you have once obtained, and you expect to get the same every other time you perform the actions. I guess you have some words to describe a scenario like this one.

It could be a process that produced information, manufactured goods, provided services or probably one that provided input for another operation. Yes, anything that requires you to redo your actions, process, efforts, observation, confirmation, testing, and so on. It is a continuous process.

You may well be achieving the expected results all the time in line with your desires. However, the effort you are putting in could be draining you because you need to do the same thing repeatedly to get the same result. It may not mean much if it were a simple process or the time involved is negligible. It is disturbing to know that many people wear themselves out to achieve the same thing. I know that so many people dread the feeling of having to do again what they have done once because it is complex, demanding, exhausting, tiring, complicated, prone to error, or frustrating. They have continued in some cases, achieving less with more. What is the way out?

Impressive goals achieved will require more to keep the same outcome and produce more. Consider a product that took so much time to complete, but you were satisfied by the result. You now desperately desire to do more but time, as some say, is not their friend. I can do more, you say, but there is no time. It is a desire that a day has 30 hours instead of 24 hours, a wish for the clock to come to a pause or a hope that the speed at which it ticks drastically reduces so that you can get more done in the same space of time. Have you ever found yourself in such a situation? You know what to do, you know how to do it, you know when to do it, you know what the outcome of all your efforts and actions would be, you are happy with the result expected, you are glad to put in all the effort required, but time is just not sufficient. What would you do?

At some point in your life, you must have written a test or examination or some form of assessment where you had a fixed time to complete the required tasks. You may be preparing for one at the moment or have some to sit for in the future. There are so many of these assessments that we face from childhood to adulthood. It could be school, trade, work, safety, professional, compliance or any other in life that evaluation is required. Everyone participating in an assessment will usually have the same amount of time to complete the tasks, and the time allocated is finite.

There was a Council report that revealed some findings on student testing. According to the report, a student takes an average of 112 tests between preschool and high school in the urban school districts surveyed. It also found that students sat for Tests over 6,570 times in one school year.[1] It will be practically impossible to go through life without understanding and facing the challenge of the limitation of time.

Time is limited for any test or assessment. It may not be pleasant to be in an examination hall when you do not know what to do. Boring it would be if you have no idea of what is required and frustrating if you do not know the answers.

Can you imagine a situation where you know all the answers, but you cannot complete the tasks in the limited time set? That is not good news. It could even be more painful, frustrating and discouraging. If it translates to failure or poor performance, there may not be a difference between the former and latter student. The outcome or success, in this case, is the ability to deliver on time; otherwise, the result will represent a lack of the required capability to succeed.

Life could be that way. You may know what to do, how, and when to do it. That sounds great. You may rightly predict the results that would attend to all your efforts and actions. It still depends on one major factor, the ability to complete all required before that last second of the test. Unfortunately, it is not always the reality for so many people today as they still have more to do when the time is over. Whenever the task required does not complete on time, the result will be different because the available or set time would have elapsed. How can you maximise time, fit more in, or do more in fixed time?

Have you ever completed the same tasks or series of activities and desired that the results were the same? You can discover some tips that can help you with some of the things you have to do and engage tools that will work for you to produce the same or better results with reduced time. This concept can increase your productivity and allow you to reach more people. It can empower you to do more with less, producing the same results even after your last action. You may finally be able to recover your time to do more crucial and often neglected things in your life that you may have long desired to do. The good news is that it will not be at the expense of your results.

Have you wondered why some organisations produce phenomenal results with fewer people and in less time? 80% of the world uses YouTube today. Two billion users can access this video platform from anywhere, through the internet, to view over 400 hours of new videos available every minute, plus over 800 million hours of videos already on it.[2] This service started fifteen years ago; today, four out of five people in the world make use of it. They were able to overtake many organisations within a short time, reaching more with less. Many more have figured this out and are doing more with less.

You may finally discover the power that is changing the world we live in and how many people, organisations, and nations are taking advantage of this concept. Many are still wondering and have no idea or clue as to what is happening. Many people have lost their jobs and means of livelihood; they are still wondering why. Some people seek relevance and employment with some expertise or skills; they seem to be frustrated as they cannot make headway because their skills are no longer required. There is a constant complaint of more to do, but far fewer skills, time or money to get it done.

Nations and organisations are going backwards instead of forward economically. They cannot figure out the reason. Many national services cannot cope with demand, as the skills required are in short supply or sometimes not even available within reasonable reach. Big businesses are folding up as they cannot compete with the market. New services are gaining ground and replacing many that have thrived for generations. Some still wonder and sigh; what is going on? What is happening? Relevance and prominence have shifted from the traditional and well known to the untraditional, new and uncommon, but unfortunately, many people are still not aware of what is happening.

I will like to introduce you, in the simplest way possible, to the world of automation. Regardless of your background, I hope this will be simple and easy enough for you and anyone to understand the power of automation. I desire that you will be able to apply the concepts to make the world a better place, thus making the most of life.

I hope you will find this insightful and helpful.

CHAPTER 1

The Place

One of the considerations for continuous success is locating the right place. It does apply to anything that would thrive, whether living or non-living things. Human beings have a lot of prospects, but for that potential to have an opportunity for expression and development, they need exposure to the right conditions. The environment does not replace the potential but allows it to perform.

A human will struggle in the water and can only survive there for a limited time. There are just too many things they cannot do because of the limitations they have in that place. So the focus is generally to skillfully breathe or fight for life for a short period because if you do not learn the skill, you may not come out alive.

On land, the case is different, as you can be there without doing anything extraordinary to be alive. You can sleep, wake up, eat, drink, move, and so on. It requires nothing outside of the ordinary, so he can use the potential to do something worthwhile.

There are also different places on land where people can flourish; some are more favourable than others. But, possibly, people need help understanding this, hence struggle because they have not found the right match of environment for their skills, gifts, specialisation, areas, or field of human endeavour.

There is a place for everything, and pursuing success will lead to frustration until that place is discovered and inhabited.

A camel can survive on land just like many land animals, but the other animals cannot face the challenges of the desert with only desert plants and no water. The success of the camel in the desert is not a function of desire but because of its makeup. It can survive without water for a long time because it can store more water than other animals. They could take in up to 145 litres of water at a single opportunity.[1] They can also eat desert plants—with sharp spines and tough leaves, which could be coarse and inedible to other animals.[2] Not many animals can wander into the desert and live. It will not matter whatever opportunities it may present because they would not even live to enjoy it—the place does not have what they need to stay alive. The choice to settle there is the beginning of their death.

You may understand why some people are struggling while others are flourishing or perhaps sense why some toil while others keep progressing effortlessly. You may see why some people are crushed by heat and lack of resources while others take advantage of the limited resources and convert it into treasure.

It may seem impressive to relocate a fish to a lovely dry land. However, the fish will begin to struggle as soon as it is out of water. The fight for its life commences, but it is only for a limited time, except there is help to get back in the water.

Some people are in a similar situation; they are alive but struggling to breathe in a toxic environment. Every other thing becomes useless and irrelevant; the swimming skills, the ability to manoeuvre, the diving skills, or the ability to sense predators. The wrong environment has made them worthless, and they could not help the fish.

The same is true for some frustrated people; they have gifts but need assistance because something needs fixing. They probably know that the idea works, or has worked for some people or used to work, but they are yet to realise the importance of where it used to work. The decision to make uninformed changes may have brought about unexplainable frustration.

The attempt to help a goat to live a better and more affluent life by moving it to a warm pool of water is not only the end but the beginning of torture and frustrating death. The difference is the environment—as simple as it may seem.

Having a hippopotamus balance nicely or gently settling on a tree branch may look good. Nice thought, but deadly consequences. Frustration, death, fatality, danger, and disaster could be some of the expected experiences. So what is it that made it so? Why is it a struggle to manage the change you so lovingly desire for them? It is the wrong place. The habitat is crucial to the survival of many things we see around us.

In the same way, it is essential to understand the influence of the territory. There is a suitable location for everything to flourish: its environment.

You do not need so much to frustrate a bird; put it in the wrong environment; even if it survives, all the potential becomes dormant and never benefits anyone.

It may surprise many, but some people expect to thrive but must realise that they have chosen to settle where their potential cannot blossom. The freedom to choose has made many choose bondage without knowing it instead of freedom and fulfilment.

Understanding and locating the right environment become a crucial part of life. It is an essential lesson in providing solutions—it may not work everywhere, so know where it works and stay there.

Automation can only work in the right environment; otherwise, it becomes dormant and unfruitful. To make things work, you need to understand where they work and ensure they are always in the right place. Automation, as powerful and effective as it may be, strongly relies on the concept of the environment.

Everything has a place where they can maximise their potential. Indeed, some may still need to maximise it, but they even have fewer or no chance in the wrong environment. A man who chooses to avoid running on land will not have a better prospect if he tries it in the air. A student who refuses to jump on the ground will be frustrated when he chooses to do so in water. He has the ability but can only enhance it in the right environment.

If you want things to work and keep working, you should always obey the law of the environment. If you don't, you have set a death date. It would only be a matter of time—a disaster is waiting to happen.

◆◆◆◆❖◆◆◆◆

There is a place for everything.

◆◆◆◆❖◆◆◆◆

CHAPTER 2

The Platform

I once bought software some years ago; like any other computer program, it comes with a manual. Many people may take it for granted, but it provides vital instruction and is a replicable concept for delivering solutions.

You will notice that it contains many details, including where to install it, where it can work and where it is not likely to work. You may wonder why they have to provide such details, but they are simply introducing the environment in which their product can flourish. If you want to make the most of the product, it is crucial to follow that guideline; otherwise, you may have a frustrating experience.

You may have discovered that some new software works in old environments. You may have some listed as a good environment, implying anything outside the list is not recommended. You may also have, in some cases, a list of the recommended and not recommended so that you make the right choice. For example, the environment could be the operating system that houses the application and helps it fulfil its functions and work to its full potential. If the operating system is incompatible, the application becomes unusable in that environment, no matter how expensive it may be.

The operating system is sound, and the application has no problem. Yes, both products are perfect in their own right, but the problem arises when someone decides that the application should work in the operating system, which will frustrate its ability. It is that combination that produces disaster and frustration.

Microsoft Office 2000, a word processing application, will not work on a computer running Windows 10, for instance. But, of course, they are products from the same company; they carry the logo of the same company, and many people are using the two products worldwide without any problems. All of that is good information, which is fine, but it does not replace the necessary conditions designed to help them function.

No matter how often you call them for help or how frustrated you feel, the only advice they can give you is to read the guidelines and use the product by adhering to the suitable and recommended conditions. The product is alright; the operating system is also not faulty. The problem lies in putting the two together and expecting them to work.

The frustration could be more significant when the attempt is to install it on devices that do not even have any operating system or those that cannot recognise it exists.

It is the first consideration because it determines whether a product will be accepted or rejected. It decides what will work and what will not. It carries the characteristics and properties that the other programs need to work.

No environment, no success. If you want a product to succeed, you need to pay close attention to what the product needs and the place that has it to give so that the product can do well. The various electronic devices we use, like Desktop computers, servers, laptops, tablets, and phones, usually come with an operating system. It could be Microsoft Windows 11, Ubuntu, CentOS, or Red Hat products, among many other options. The operating system creates the environment which determines the success of anything that will run on it.

You probably have had some problems with your computer, software, devices, or peripherals and found that even though you have a working printer, you got the sad news that it would not work with your computer.

They must have told you that the software you bought and love so much cannot work on your device. You must have gotten the news that the app you found cannot go on your device. You probably figured it out after so many painful trials and searches that the software or application for which you bought a new and shiny machine will not work after all. You found that even though it is excellent and faultless as a product, it does not guarantee that it can work anywhere. Something determines its success which is the environment.

It explains the frustration of so many people today; they work so hard with exceptional abilities and potential but struggle in the wrong place. It is hard, but it would only work in the right place.

I discovered that so much is invested in operating systems to make all the devices work well. Some additional work goes in to improve the place for any new device. You may have found that drivers get installed to help the new device communicate properly. Regular updates also help improve the environment to make it a conducive and optimal place for all that depend on it. The importance and relevance of the operating system make it worth the level of investment it commands.

Many things will fail, not because they are faulty but because the environment is. It is sad to know, but a good product in the wrong place will produce a poor result.

We know the place for many things and can see them flourish there, but many are yet to find their place.

Where should you be to flourish?

The boat needs water to function and succeed as a boat. The plant must be in the soil; the fish must be in the water to thrive. The birds must be in the air. It is not a luxury; it is a necessity. Therefore, it would be best if you found your place.

CHAPTER 3

The Chance

There are so many factors that determine the success of an idea. Some are indeed more important than others in the lifecycle of the concept.

It is like a living thing—a plant or animal. They cannot live when some factors are not there. They will not thrive without others, while the absence of some others may only show as a deficiency or deprive them of reaching their maximum potential.

A fish cannot live without water, but with water, they have more chances of growing and reaching maturity as they could function to get the other things they need. A tree needs the soil; when it becomes disconnected from the earth, it begins to dry, no matter how much nutrients you provide. It can only benefit from the nutrient in the soil. No matter the nutrients or food available, a goat cannot survive in water. It needs to be on land to benefit from the nourishment that will make it grow.

Some time ago, a baby whale which measured about 4m in length, washed ashore and was stranded as it got stuck in the River Thames in London. Finding a minke whale in the river hundreds of miles from home was strange. Although it was still in the water—shallow waters were not quite like its home, so the hope of surviving there was pretty slim. The experts concluded that the only way was to return the young mammal to sea as it cannot survive without the benefits its habitat provides. The mission to help the animal was not successful as the rescuers would have loved. Sadly whatever it was that made it deviate to the wrong environment has caused its death.[1]

The environment is effective and could determine the chance to succeed or survive. So many people need help not because they are not in a domain but the wrong one. They could be in familiar territory; even if the difference is just the shallow waters, it is different enough to frustrate every effort to progress and greatly diminish the chance to succeed. The minke was still in the water but not in suitable waters.

The stories of whales getting washed ashore get reported in the news; most are seen dead. Whatever prompted the change has caused unrecoverable damage.

In December 2020, the BBC reported the deaths of ten sperm whales on Christmas eve, trapped between Tunstall and Withernsea. A spokesperson described it as a tragedy. According to British Divers Marine Life Rescue members, a navigation error was one of the reasons for such tragedy.[2]

The animal did not change; only the environment did. There is something more in the habitat that makes the whale flourish with less effort that is not present in the new location. It explains many tragic situations we see; it could simply be because of a change, simple, little but with significant implications. Whatever lures you away from where you can flourish could lead to a disaster and significantly reduces your chances and prospects. Your environment has much to do with your growth, development, and maximizing your potential. You get the resources, guidance, and teaching to make you what you need to be and help to maximize your potential. It seems to work, but it is because you are in a supportive and necessary environment for your development.

If you know the environment you need, it is almost 50% of success already. You then need to understand what you can fit into and the relationships between the environment and what you want to bring into it. It would help if you found the environment that will make you flourish and quit the environment that would frustrate you to death. The environment is not dangerous because it is poisonous to all. It is not your environment because it does not provide the necessities for your development and flourishing. Remember, the whale was still in the water, which is suitable for many water animals to grow, but the whale needs more. It requires the capacity its habitat will provide. The whale cannot thrive in the same place even though it is not dangerous or toxic to other animals.

Man can swim in water for some time, but to live in water, he cannot live to his full potential. Water may not have poisonous substances, but it does not have what man needs to flourish and maximize potential. Do you have the maximum chance to succeed and maximize your potential? First, you should check that you are in the right environment. You have a better prospect when you are where all the resources you need to flourish are available. Then, you can grow and develop naturally, and every effort you put in will produce significant and noticeable results. You can make your efforts worthwhile by ensuring you are in the right environment. If you are not, you can make the change that will give you a chance to succeed.

CHAPTER 4

The Dormant

Many people may never realise their potential because they need help finding the environment to enable them to flourish. They have potential, but it does not produce because it has yet to come in contact with the resources that will allow them to become fruitful. Interestingly, the potential remains there while they continue to experience frustration and no fulfilment. Some may never see the realisation of what they carry because they have lost hope, not knowing what to do. However, if they understand and believe in what they have, they may be encouraged to find the place crucial for their development.

A dry seed will remain dormant even though it can become a plant or tree that will bear fruit. It depends on where it is. If you keep it dry, safe, and secure, it will remain that way and never develop into a plant, nor will it produce fruit, although it can do so. When you decide to plant it and change the environment, giving it access to the resources and help it needs, you will begin to see the hidden potential that has always been there. It would break through the shell and manifest into a plant growing to produce fruits. The environment can bring a significant change when you realise and decide to make the change that will bring fruitfulness and fulfilment.

Some years ago, Dr Sarah Sallon, an Israeli scientist and the director of the Borick Natural Medicine Research Center at Hadassah University Hospital, discovered many seeds in the country's archaeological sites. Still, only a little got done with them except for examination, but she thought to go further to find the potential of the seeds.[1] Something hidden in them has yet to find an opportunity for release. The prospect was waiting and longing for expression.

A phenomenal discovery found hundreds of seeds in a prehistoric palace constructed in the first century BC by King Herod the Great. They were in a bone-dry environment and had been in the same state for over 2000 years.[2] The seeds were there for many generations but could not release any potential because the environment was not conducive for them to do so.

Dr Sallon did have hope in the seeds and made a significant change as she collected some of them and decided to change their environment to help release the potential. She worked with Dr Elaine Solowey, a horticulturist that manages the Center for Sustainable Agriculture at the Arava Institute for Environmental Studies at Kibbutz Ketura. Their efforts were successful as they germinated some of the seeds, eventually growing to become a tree that produced fruits. It is interesting to note, as they say, is the oldest Judean date seed ever germinated.[3] It retained its characteristics for 2000 years and could still release the potential with the same qualities when relocated to a conducive environment.

The most awesome favour you can do to any living thing is to take it back to its environment. The most excellent solution you can offer to anything is to ensure they find the domain they have been designed to function. In the same way, the tremendous help you can do to anyone is to help them find their place, the environment where they can thrive, find fulfilment, and where things can work for them with diminished involvement. People would struggle less when they see their place. Things are working like automation is at work because the potential has stumbled on the right resources, and natural growth becomes the result.

I can imagine the reaction of the seed when the environment changes. It will begin to sense what it has never felt for 2000 years. The dormant power was let loose, and newness broke through all barriers. The seed that should have produced trees and fruits for many generations was lying idle in the king's palace. It is similar to the experience of so many people. The years keep going by, but they remain the same: no progress, growth, or power. It may be an issue with the environment.

Some people have lost hope, seen as nobody; all they need is a change, enabling environment, someone that could refine and support them, or a community that could help appreciate and nourish their hidden gifts. Then, they will flourish after so many years of dryness and fruitlessness. It is like magic. When the seed lands in an enabling environment—packed with the nourishment it needs to develop—it will begin to activate that dormant potential. They were not dead; they were only static.

What do you need to thrive? What do you need to bring out the best in you? The discovery would be the greatest secret kept from you.

Can you imagine a man that has potential but remains dormant for many years? Some people may be alive, but their potential never got activated because they never found the place that could make them grow.

The change you expect in yourself or others may only become a reality once you initiate a change of environment. Yet, there is something within everyone longing for the power of the right place.

Many people have become victims of the wrong place, they have only lived a shadow of themselves, but there is hope because they can find their home and give life to those dormant seeds. They are not dead; they are only static, longing for help.

CHAPTER 5

The Compatible

Every manufacturer designs a product to work and function in a particular environment. For example, a car is for driving on land, so it could only provide its best on the ground. The parts of the vehicle can work well on land. The tyre touches the ground and can move when operated, even driven at high speeds on the road. Likewise, the ship is for the water, so you can only appreciate what it can do in that environment. The parts of the vessel will work well in water and be stable. When operated, it can move on the water with the maximum weight specified by the manufacturer.

If you attempt to use a car in the water, there will be a problem; the car will not be able to work as the operation negates the design, so it will not perform as expected. Furthermore, it will only struggle for a while and get destroyed. It is not because the car is unreliable; it is because the car's abilities by design had a particular environment in mind, which informs the manufacturer's decision to recommend its use on land.

You can do anything you like with what you have, but that action could destroy the product and waste the in-built potential. Hence, understanding compatibility is crucial to the product's success. The product can function to its maximum potential in an environment where other resources, possibly other products, can work together to achieve a common goal while allowing the individual inbuilt function to have free expression.

One of the models of the cars built by Ford is called Focus. It requires fuel to run, but not just any type can work to make it function because there is a particular specification by design. There is a tank already prepared to store it. It is just a container; in reality, it can hold any liquid, but only the compatible substance will help the car function as expected. The car is built to recognise and accept compatible products and could function and flourish using them in line with the manufacturer's design. The vehicle has a recommended fuel, unleaded petrol, and everyone who desires to use the car should use the fuel type so the vehicle can continue to run as designed. If it is not compatible, it could lead to the destruction of the product.

The software must be compatible with a computer's or device's operating system to work as expected. The operating system cannot function at its best without compatibility with the device's hardware. Therefore, if any software would work without the intervention, it should be in an environment where it can work together and function with other related software.

In the same way, the concept of compatibility is applied in automation to allow different products to function as designed because they have been recommended by the manufacturers and proven compatible. In other words, they would work together, stay together, or function individually and collectively to their maximum potential.

For instance, Microsoft PowerShell can automate tasks and is supported and compatible with some Windows operating systems. Furthermore, the two can live together, so if you want to automate tasks, you can use PowerShell, create your commands, and they will get executed.

If you can get PowerShell to understand what you want to do, you can then present them in the form of commands, and then it would get the operating system to execute them while you no longer need to be there. You can do it once and let it continue to work while you can engage your time doing something else.

Any product compatible with the same or similar software can achieve the same result. The simple idea is that the compatibility of the products forms the basis for the possibility of automation. If they can work together, you can take advantage of that relationship to achieve your goal.

A rollercoaster works as designed. It can move dozens of people comfortably on chairs attached to a metal base. They move in different directions, controlled by a button. It is because many products that could work together were put together in a specific way to accomplish the feat. So you would see wires, sensors, and motors, among other components, strategically located in the design to help do the work without needing any intervention. The compatibility of the products made it possible so that they can each perform the individual function and work together to accomplish the joint goal. The understanding of compatibility provides countless opportunities to offer solutions based on automation.

Metals can move on a wheel in a circular motion. It could be a simple solution connecting to an electronic panel that will trigger the motor to roll. It can solve some problems; for example, cows can be moved around on the metal to feed, milk, or achieve other goals. You can achieve automation in the farm by moving cows using electronics attached to the metal. The two different components can work together through the concept of compatibility.

The automatic kettle is possible because various components work together and communicate in a suitable environment. For example, the thermostat has a characteristic property that responds to temperature changes which communicates with a switch to power off the kettle when it reaches the programmed temperature.

You can create an environment where the various parts can communicate and work together. But first, you need to understand your needs and find the best environment to support or help you.

The key is finding the functions you have and making them work together to achieve your goal. The right environment for a thing will make provision for all the functioning parts to work together to achieve the common goal.

◆◆◆◆❖◆◆◆◆

If it is not compatible, it could lead to the destruction of the product.

◆◆◆◆❖◆◆◆◆

CHAPTER 6

The Simulation

One of the ways to solve problems is to restore order where there is a problem, chaos, or disorder. When things are not in their proper place, there is disorder, and when items do not have what they need to function, there is also a problem.

The car needs the road, an essential resource to function and maximise its potential. If the car is good, but the road is terrible, there is a problem, and an attempt to fix the problem will be an effective solution to prolong the car's life. Understanding compatibility will help you bring compatible things together, thus creating solutions to make things work and supporting each product to maximise its potential.

A train needs a track; transportation would still be a problem if one is unavailable. There could be trains available but unable to service the people that need them in some locations because of the lack of a suitable train track. The track is necessary as part of the environment to support the train and thus solve the transportation problem.

I have seen boats built on land, but when they want to put them to use, they move them to a different environment. It is a crucial step because it can never meet the need for transportation on land, even though the design and manufacture took place on the ground. They have to transport it to the waters where it can properly function and fulfil its purpose. It could be a natural water source like a river, sea, or an artificial pool that mimics the same environment; the crucial thing is that water is sufficient for it to move.

There are so many things around us that are not in their environment, and there are so many things that we see that we cannot practically take to their natural habitat. Simulation can be very productive in designing products and providing solutions. The idea of simulation is to create the required environment with the same or similar characteristics to benefit the product.

To create the same effect, you can study the environment to understand the relationships and make something similar for the new location of the product. It is beneficial in automation because you can only sometimes have the original environment, especially if you plan for the product to work with so many other products. The good news is that you can simulate it and incorporate that into a new environment for it to function.

A seed grows on land, but if you want the plant away from land, you could simulate the environment by putting soil or compost in a vase and planting the same seed in the vase. You have brought the benefit of the ground to a different environment. It has made it possible to benefit from the goodness of the plant in a different location where the presence of soil could be minimal but yet get the benefit that it provides to the plant.

It explains why you can have a plant in your office, room, or lounge, and it will grow. You do not have to fill your office with soil like a farm, but you only bring the compatible environment in sufficient quantity to take advantage of the plant's goodness. That is the simple simulation concept; it solves problems by taking the environment in a portable simulated version closer to the product.

You can also use the same for other factors necessary for the plant to grow, like water, temperature, and light. For example, you would prefer to avoid rain coming through your living room roof, but you could provide the water that the rain shower offers for the plant. Then, when you have completed all the requirements and can cause the product to thrive and succeed in a different location, you will have provided the simulated environment for it to release its full potential.

The car needs a power source to run but cannot be tied to a power source and fulfil its transportation function. How can that be achieved? A battery is a simulation of the power that can move along with the car to perform its function. The car battery gets charged as it gets used using a system that provides the charge on the motion. So the vehicle can move from one place to another instead of being tied to a spot, enjoying the same power benefits. The mobile solution lets you benefit from other portable electronic devices and entertainment. So many products have benefited from wireless technology because of the introduction of a simulated environment. It has made it possible to provide more solutions without the need to stay tied to one location. You may also think of more examples, including mobile phones, wireless hair trimmers or clippers, torches, laptops, tablets, and so on. They are all products that function anywhere because the manufacturers incorporated a simulated environment that could help them function.

The zoo provides an environment for all kinds of animals, making it possible to see and study the animals in a controlled manner. Moreover, it makes it possible for many animals from different habitats to live close enough to achieve a particular purpose: education, preservation, or tourist attraction.

An artificial pond can be an option when created with similar characteristics to the habitat of a tilapia fish. It is possible to achieve the same water concentration and nutrient requirements far from the natural habitat or location. The focus is the fish, and the aim is to bring all the essentials into a constructed environment to help them flourish just as they would in their natural habitat.

When adopted in automation, this concept would help provide outstanding solutions where there seem to be impossibilities.

In computer technology, software like firmware and drivers help to make one product work with another. It is the same concept of environment. For example, a mouse can work with a computer to perform its function because software can help them work together. However, you may have noticed that a new device will only work when attached to a computer once the driver or software gets installed. In order words, the conditions to make it function are necessary for it to work in the new environment.

You can connect a printer to a computer physically, but it may not work when you decide to print, or it may need to be recognised as they may not be able to communicate, let alone function together. The printer needs its environment, so the manufacturer packages the software with the product. It is a portable version of the environment that you can take with you wherever you decide to use the product. If your product comes with a mobile environment that makes it usable in almost any location or with many other products, it will usually increase the value of your product.

The advancement in computer technology has made it possible to use different products on different devices, and it seems seamless because of the portability of the environment. A mouse can work by connecting it to a USB port on any computer. A camera will function when connected to a laptop. A microphone, speaker, scanner, bar code reader, printer, joystick, and headphones, among others, can work together with a computer or other compatible device to perform their function. They can do so in a different location because the new environment also has a simulation of what their environment provides for them to function.

You will find that many problems will get solved quickly by taking every product as close as possible to its environment or simulating the characteristics it needs and ensuring it is available in the new environment.

Automation, in most cases, depends on many products working together, communicating, and collaborating. But, of course, it is not impossible for different things—with various qualities and characteristics to work together even if they are miles away from their environment. The key to such a feat is understanding the importance of the environment in their success and ensuring you can satisfy each product's environmental need and bring it as close as possible to its new environment.

◆◆◆◆❖◆◆◆◆

The simple simulation concept; it solves problems by taking the environment in a portable simulated version closer to the product.

◆◆◆◆❖◆◆◆◆

CHAPTER 7

The Project

Have you ever wondered why some certain animals are only in certain places? Do you know why some plants only grow in some countries?

Every living thing has needs, and it is essential to get what they need to thrive. The place that provides them is where you can find them; they would enjoy being there. They will do well in their location because all they need to flourish is available there. It represents the cumulation or the pool of resources that support their daily need.

You may also have found this accurate, but still wonder if you can have them at easy reach without the need to travel for hours to get to their original habitat.

Can you bring them closer to enjoy the same benefit without putting them at risk?

We often get new experiences as we try new things and visit new places. One of the likely possibilities is that we may have a desire; having seen or eaten a fruit or vegetable for the first time away from home, we want the experience to continue. However, we have often heard discouraging words that indicate that we should not try because it only grows in a particular place. In order words, you must always go there if you want the experience again.

The taste of discovery and the feeling of it must not end here, met with a statement of disappointment and cruel reality. Can you relate to such an encounter?

I know some people would not even take no for an answer; they will give it a try regardless to satisfy their curiosity. For example, a young man saw a fruit that appealed to him, and after eating it, he decided to keep the seed to plant it in his home county. He was hopeful, but unfortunately, it did not grow. It does not respond to hope but to the right conditions— the young man found after the experiment.

I have also attempted similar experiments whenever I ate or saw a new fruit, vegetable, or plant that I liked. I find the seed or the stem so I can take it away and plant it in a different location. It worked for some years, and I could enjoy the plants as they grew in our garden, where I had easy access and could benefit from them at easy reach. I did this in the same region for many years and continued to see excellent results. However, I later discovered that it is only sometimes the case, as some plants will only flourish in an environment that will enable them to grow.

I once tried to grow a vegetable plant that flourishes in a tropical climate, but it did not survive when I planted it in a temperate climate. The plant was perfect, and I planted it in the soil, but some things were missing in the environment required for it to flourish. The plant did not enjoy the climate; it never survived, even with enough water, manure, and other favourable conditions. I learned that you could not just plant anything anywhere and expect it to maximize its potential. Instead, I discovered that plants need their unique environment, and whoever desires to move them must fully understand the essentials they need. When they get uprooted from their environment and planted in an unfavourable one, they will not flourish; they will die after some time.

Many people have moved plants or animals from their environment and found out the truth the hard way. They tried to relocate an animal from one place to another but only discovered that they died. So many people like me have taken plants they liked so they could grow them in their garden in a different country but found it would not work. It could be frustrating when everything else seems fine, but they cannot just survive because of the one essential condition of the new place. I almost concluded that it could not happen but still pondered how to make it work.

Then, some years later, I visited the Eden Project in Cornwall. Furthermore, for the first time, I saw crops growing far away from where they are known to produce—thriving in a place with significant environmental differences. I have never seen it before, but I saw it there.

It was fascinating as you could see tropical plants bearing fruits and thriving in a country with a different and unfavourable climate. It will intrigue you to see cacao, banana, pineapple, arabica coffee, oil palm, sugar cane, Baobab, plantain, and various plants flourishing.

It was an experience akin to walking into a different country and enjoying the benefit of two worlds.

I spent some time looking at and asking questions about the environment within. Then, finally, I discovered that making an environment similar or as close as possible to its original climate was possible.

All they did was simulate the environment where the plants can thrive, which has been a success there for many years. They found the right temperature and replicated the same using a heating system in enclosed huge biome buildings even though the natural temperature was still colder. It has made it possible for over one thousand varieties of tropical plants to thrive and bear fruit as they would in their original climate.[1] The idea of matching temperature and moisture levels to what obtains in the tropical environment provided a significant breakthrough. It made it possible to see plants grow even in a simulated environment. The plants did not notice; they grew as long as it was right. The same plants that only grow in Africa can also thrive in Europe, using the same technology. It will no longer matter if it is thousands of miles away. It would no longer be necessary whether it is snowing or freezing. The investment to keep the environment constant will help the plants to flourish.

There is so much information and strategic lessons to learn from it. When you want a plant or animal to thrive in a different place, you must try to understand the environment and do all you can to replicate or simulate it.

It has brought enlightenment about the possibility of leaving one environment for a dissimilar one and yet achieving success. Of course, you could accomplish the same anywhere if you get the same environment or a simulated one with all the necessary characteristics. However, if those criteria never get fulfilled in the new place, it is almost guaranteed that the plant will only experience the termination of its life.

It is crucial to note all conditions in the location when you see things that thrive and plants that flourish, much more than the potential within them, which is, of course, necessary, but also the place conducive for releasing that potential.

Do you want to start a new thing that will flourish, and you cannot practically go to the environment? Then, there is an option to learn about the environment and bring the location or simulate it so your product or idea can have a place to flourish. An unfavourable area can kill a dream; it can destroy a future, do not take it for granted. Please only move your idea once the conditions favour growth.

Some people underestimate the conditions because they have never had to move, relocate, expand or change, so they benefit from the same conditions as a default. But, unfortunately, the success will not continue when they decide to change. The reality will only dawn on some people after some unpleasant experience, but you can avoid the errors and plan. The need is an environment that will favour your seed or plant, causing it to thrive.

One thing is sure, if you get rewards or fruits because your ideas grow, one among many other factors—the environment was right, intentionally or otherwise, but if it is not conducive, it will not be a pleasant experience. So get it in the right place and get it right.

◆◆◆◆❖◆◆◆◆

You could not just plant anything anywhere and expect it to maximize its potential

◆◆◆◆❖◆◆◆◆

CHAPTER 8

The Function

Some years ago, one organisation upgraded all their computer systems to keep up with the latest version. They used the computers for different purposes, but some had to connect them to other devices like printers, scanners, barcode readers, or other devices—for example, one piece of scientific equipment connected to a computer system. Still, the computer system was due for an upgrade, and the recommendation was to have a newer and better computer to connect to the equipment.

The scientist was okay with the idea as long as they could continue their work and use the equipment. The project was well underway, with procurement for the new systems and a replacement plan already in place. It was going on successfully as most of the recipients of the new systems could do their work on the new system.

As the project progressed, it was time to replace the computer attached to the scientific equipment. The replacement happened, and everything looked good and better. However, there was a problem only briefly after the scientists decided to test the new setup. They found that it was not working. However, they thought it was probably an easy fix, so they called the engineers to have a look to help resolve the issue.

They could have only wished it was an easy fix, but they found that it could not work with the equipment after some hours of trying. They contacted the manual for information and spoke to the distributor and the manufacturer. They sought a solution and information on how to get it to work. Unfortunately, they painfully discovered that their success in helping every other person with a new computer would not happen in this laboratory. The new computer is not supported and cannot work with this equipment. A new computer cannot work, yes, because the equipment cannot work with that computer, the environment is strange, and it could not identify the features or communicate in such a way as to perform its function.

That is interesting. There is a bigger problem with finding a suitable replacement for the computer system. The computer would not work with the equipment nor recognise or communicate with it.

What is the solution? They were so many suggestions and attempts, but they needed help to get an easy answer to make the new system work. They now suggested that it is about time they get rid of the old equipment and buy a new one that could work with the new computer. That would be a good solution, they thought. They presented the idea to the scientists, but the scientist smiled and said the equipment cost more than one million pounds. The computer is less than one thousand pounds, should we get rid of the equipment for a new computer? They opined.

The value of the equipment was more than the computer, and instead of getting rid of a one million pound equipment, they would prefer their old systems as long as it worked.

The value of the equipment and the function is more critical than getting a new enticement that will not work or function.

I was fascinated by their choice, and it could help so many people in such a situation struggling to choose an environment that will help them function. The new system is excellent, but they could not sacrifice the role of a million-pound equipment for a new device. In order words, their purpose and function as a department rely on that expensive equipment, but a new device will only offer cosmetic value if it cannot help or support their primary function. So they chose to continue to function instead of changing to something new that would cause them to cease functioning.

The environment provides not just a place, connection, or accommodation; it provides the resources to function, flourish, and maximise potential and purpose.

Many places can accommodate a mango seed, but not all can help them grow. Likewise, a tiger can physically fit into many places, but not all can help nourish and make it grow to its best. However, there is a place that provides what they need to grow and flourish and fulfil their function. It is the place that accommodates them and helps them perform as designed. It gives significance and provides resources to accomplish their role, not just for fancy or providing cosmetic value.

Many have decided, unlike the scientists mentioned earlier, to get a new computer system that will render useless scientific equipment worth over one million pounds.

Why? They think of new, better, fancy, beauty, cosmetics, people's opinion, latest, and fashionable, but neglect the impact on the ability to function and thrive.

A few years ago, we visited a farm in Bern, Switzerland. I saw pigs, among other animals, on the farm. A dozen piglets surrounded a boar and sow. They were all having fun, playing in the mud. It may look unpleasant, especially when you need to understand why they find joy in such a place. They need it, and the environment that provides such adds value. They would achieve a different result in a decorated area full of fancy-looking and expensive jewellery pieces. They need that value to perform their function, and the place that provides it is crucial to their growth and development. I found that pigs do not have as many sweat glands as humans do, and the few do not function in the same way; hence they cannot sweat like humans but rely on wallowing to prevent overheating when the temperature rises.[1]

Can you imagine a place; fancy, gorgeous, and expensive? A purpose-built house, well decorated with precious metals and adorned with the most pricey accessories you could think of or have come across. Yes, you would have loved the description and decided to make it your choicest place, but when told it will prevent you from sweating or passing out waste, you may have to pause to think again. Consider the value it would add if it prevents you from such an essential function. What is the value of a place that would not allow you to release waste? It would only contribute to your destruction. It is excellent, fancy, expensive, and all gold, but for you, it would lead to your doom or cause you to malfunction and lead to your end.

The value of wallowing to the pig is much more than what a different environment would provide. It helps, among other things, to achieve the social function necessary for their well-being and development.[2] It is not about how cheap or expensive. It is about the value it provides them to function and achieve their potential and purpose.

Many times people mistake getting the most expensive for what they need. It is costly does not mean you need it. It is new, fashionable, and well-known, but it may not help you. Some have frustrated their progress by exchanging their environment for one that offers cosmetic value. They have destroyed their future by choosing based on looks, opinions of others, familiarity, or fashionable instead of function.

Whatever environment does not help you grow and reach your potential is destructive, no matter how expensive it may be or respected it may be in the opinion of others. It is destroying you, frustrating your potential, and killing your abilities. If you are still waiting to realise that, you may have lost value for the function. The joy and fulfilment of a pig in the right environment cannot compare to any other. You will lose something crucial to you until you find the best environment. It is not money, beauty, elegance, fame, or fortune; it is fulfilment. When fulfilment is more critical, the domain that helps you achieve that will be more important. When you make that choice, you have chosen to value function because it determines your sense of value for the environment.

Many places can accommodate you, but only a few can transform you.

Some may tolerate or abuse your potential, but there is an environment that will unleash it.

CHAPTER 9

The Engrafted

A fruit tree is usually known to bear one type of fruit. For example, if you plant a mango seed, it becomes a mango tree that produces mango fruits—like oranges, pears, or plums. However, I learned many years ago of a technique of vegetative propagation that makes it possible for two plant tissues to join together and continue to grow, retaining their characteristics. It is grafting, and it helps achieve the result of more than one fruit from one tree. A fruit tree's lower rootstock portion joins the scion portion of another variety of fruit trees.

Using this technique, you can have different varieties of oranges on the same tree instead of just one type. Why is it possible for another tree to join another tree and yet still grow and also produce its fruit? The environment is compatible and could help it flourish and functions like its environment.

This technique could help in many ways and could be applied to achieve excellent results.

Sam Van Aken, an art professor, pushed this further as he grew one tree that can produce up to forty different stone fruits or fruit with pits. The list of fruits includes peaches, apricots, plums, cherries, and nectarines. He achieved this by cutting the buds from different fruit trees and grafting them onto the branches of a single tree. He made what he referred to as the tree of forty fruit.[1]

It applies to many other life areas to achieve great results. For example, in computer technology and Engineering, compatible components are beneficial to produce the same effect to help the system continue to perform its function. Product manufacturers list parts compatible with the products in their product manuals. It is usually different, but it can work to make the system perform its functions.

A compatible car part from another manufacturer can replace like-for-like parts as long as they are similar in characteristics and function and accepted as a recommended replacement. If they are incompatible, they will not work or work as expected.

You are likely to have experienced some compatibility issues if you have changed or upgraded a computer device or software. For example, it could be a printer that could no longer work with a newer operating system or a device that could no longer be connected to a computer because there is no interface suitable for the connection.

Many things only work if permitted in the original design and are compatible. However, finding the same resource in a different environment can help you bring many other components together, like the fruit tree, to share the benefits of a single domain while producing different results.

The computer system could be a single environment that houses the resources for all connected devices, each performing its unique function.

A car has a system that houses all the resources and coordinates the activities of all the components attached to it, including mechanical, electrical, or electronics. The different parts could function and work during their varying functions but working together and controlled by the system. For example, you can control the tyre through the brake pedal, which communicates with the brake pads attached to the tyre's rim.

The battery in a car provides mobile and rechargeable energy that would meet all the vehicle's power needs, and it moves from one point to another. There are different types of batteries used in cars. Each car has a requirement, hence the right kind of battery. It must be compatible with the vehicle, as one that is incompatible will not work even if it is a battery or even looks similar.

Whatever you do can work when you get the environment right, even with a compatible solution, but there would be problems and frustration if you get it wrong.

What can you do when it is not practicable to attach to the original environment? Preferably, you can find a compatible solution. The concept of compatibility helps you achieve many different functions in one collaborative environment that meets the functional requirements of all the components attached.

The understanding of compatibility is beneficial in automation as it will help reduce or compact the environment, making it portable yet achieving many diverse functions from different components or systems.

That is why we can have a small computer system with diverse components working in it to give a unique experience. For example, the aeroplane has many parts that work together to make the whole unit work. The entire unit represents a moveable system that can meet the needs of every component attached. For example, the aeroplane's battery will power up the electrical system and start the engines—you will not need to hook up to a power station. The understanding of compatibility will help produce many things that could use many parts that could work together in the same portable environment.

You can save space, time, and resources by consolidating compatible resources to serve many components that produce different functions. You would have applied the same principle of grating by using the solution.

CHAPTER 10

The Enhancement

One of the lessons I learned as a student of agricultural science is the difference the environment could make to the outcome of a seed. We once had a project to plant vegetable seeds using a portion of land allotted for every class member. They were the same, distributed to everyone from the same source; the land was also the same, so everyone had an allotment from the same ground. The task was to present the vegetables when they matured in their best possible form. The assessment and the marks awarded will be based on the status of plants at the point of harvest.

There was a clear motivation to do all possible to present the plants in their best possible state at harvest time. The seed is the same; the land is the same; the question then was, what extra can one do to make a difference in the plant's life to make it the best it could become?

Every student started to work on the project, but some did more work than others. Everyone planted the seeds in the soil, but some did extra to help maximise the potential, while some did the minimum or not enough to protect their plant from emerging dangers.

Some students decided to build plant beds and added more nutrients to enrich the soil to have enough nourishment for the seeds. Cow dung was one of the free and easily accessible options, so some went for that to improve their soil. Regular watering was also a common practice to provide the essential need of the plants. There were some allotments with a protective edge around them to prevent unnecessary access to them as it was in the school compound.

It was an exciting project for young students, but the lesson was phenomenal.

In the end, the result was different, and a few stood out from the rest. Remember, everyone started with the same vegetable seed, but each allotment looked different based on what each person did to enhance their space.

The leaves of the vegetables were fresher, taller, and more prominent in a few; some looked dry and thin, some were short, and some seemed to have had more accidents and injuries because of external forces that accessed the place. It was visible on the stems and structure—they probably had a few mishaps from students playing around. I discovered that the plants that turned out the best had all the necessary things required for flourishing with adequate protection. In addition, they had essential environmental enhancements, which made them significantly different from the others.

All the allotments had plants, but the outcome was different, even with the same seed and soil. It shows that many factors can influence the environment, which could impact the seed's life and hence the outcome. The plant could benefit from enhancement by adding nutritional value; similarly, it could suffer setbacks by adding poisonous substances to the environment or removing valuable nutrients. It could suffer untimely death or injury if there is no protection against harmful external forces. The addition or subtraction of crucial benefits influences the environment and, in turn, the plant's growth pattern.

The environment will help it grow, but the influencers significantly impact it because they determine how it develops. The vegetable plant responds to enhancement or diminution.

In the same way, a good seed can produce a malnourished or diseased tree not because it is not viable but because the environment is not at its best for the plant. The fruit becomes deficient because of pests or other negative factors influencing the growth.

I have found this to be true in life as many people are affected by influencers; they grow, but the growth for some is positive, but for others, it could be damaging. All the plants were growing, but not all reached the same potential we saw at harvest. We did not see the full potential of the seeds even though they came out best because we only saw the output of the enhancement we were able to provide to the environment as young students. The same seeds could produce more in a more enhanced environment.

The power of influence is significant, and no one should think it is a good idea to ignore it. So whenever you want to change your life, check your environment—it can limit how far you can go and determine how you grow.

Some young children grow to become confident or timid because of their environment. Victims of abuse are affected by their experiences, which could result in lasting damage, except they get help quickly and gain access to an enhanced environment.

Health experts advise pregnant women not to smoke because it will influence their baby and determine how the child grows. The child does not have a problem, but something influences the baby's growth and gradually shapes the child's life. For example, a child's growth in a traumatised environment will affect him negatively. In the same way, if he is in an enhanced setting, it will have a positive impact. The child responds to the influences, whether positive or negative.

When they had their last child, a family migrated from an Anglophone country to a francophone nation. The boy grew up in the environment and could speak and communicate in French with the same accent as the indigenes. Interestingly, his parents' language was not natural to him, but that of his environment became normal. The experience would have been different if they did not relocate or created a deliberate learning environment for the desired language in the new location. It is a function of the influence of the new place they found themselves.

What you do or do not do to the environment around the seed will determine how the seed will grow. Unfortunately, many people only seem excited about how the vegetable seed grows. Still, only a few realise how it develops is equally essential and depends on environmental influences.

You can get something better, bigger, taller, more robust, and healthier if you pay more attention to the environment. Similarly, it could result in a weaker, smaller, thinner harvest when the influence is harmful, obstructive, or destructive.

Everyone can be a better version of themselves if they enhance their environment. For example, a healthy family will produce a healthy child, but a family where abuse is the order of the day will also affect the children there. A company of wise people with a positive attitude will also produce after their kind. It is an environmental influence.

You can learn how to make your environment work for you to help release your full potential. You will only get what the environment can offer if you do nothing. It could be that you are only living at the mercy of others and their inputs, but it could be positive or negative. You can be deliberate about your future and add the values that will make you flourish and fulfil your potential.

Like the young boy described earlier, a seed takes up the language or culture of its environment by default. So, if you want to improve in French, surround yourself with a french speaking community. If you desire good grades, surround yourself with high-quality materials and people with the right attitude. If you want to do well in business, join a company of people that can enhance you. If you desire to pursue your gift, surround yourself with relevant materials and a community that can enrich your dream.

You can always add value to your soil to improve the quality of your harvest. It will always produce the same way by default, except something is done to improve the situation. Then, when you decide to make deliberate changes, you have embraced the enhancement concept and will enjoy the bumper harvest. A slight enhancement can make a significant difference; the time to act is now.

◆◆◆◆❖◆◆◆◆

You can always add value to your soil to improve the quality of your harvest.

CHAPTER 11

The Constant

So many products around us work as they were designed to and have done so for many years. We see them functioning but may often overlook what makes them work or why they continue to work. In some cases, one may have seen some situations where they fail to work as expected or stop working, and you may wonder why, but there is a hint if we study the nature of the environment that hosts the product.

The environment is also affected by many other elements, which bring about change that affects the products. Therefore, the factors only sometimes seem favourable. Still, some are necessary while others are not, but it is the nature of the environment, part of the package, which implies that you can only shield or minimise the effect on your product and not get rid of all of them altogether.

Harsh is a reality of the environment that is worthy of consideration. The seed grows into a plant and experiences the differences that all seasons offer for its growth and development. Rain, wind, storm, snow, or sun rays all take turns to impact the life of the plant in their different seasons. It is sometimes cold, hot, wet, or freezing. Some plants practically go dormant because of the temperature. There are visible signs of colour changes or shrinkage, but their growth continues in favourable conditions. It is the reality of every environment. The factors are peculiar to the climate and offer some benefits too, so it must be understood to take advantage of them and be aware and guided against the challenges.

The lion in their environment hunt for food, but they usually succeed once out of every four attempts[1], but they can survive without food for up to two weeks.[2] They still have to work to get food.

The trees get exposed to the sun, which is necessary for their development, contributing positively to their growth and development. But of course, the right environment also comes with challenging times where the situation could be better, but it is a season one must be prepared to go through.

Honda, the Japanese company, produces automobiles, but they all work if they are driven on roads, regardless of the country. Some other factors affect the cars even when driven on the road. The company has considered and tested how the vehicle would react under such conditions. For example, rain, wind, heat, and cold, among others, could impact the car. The product, when built, had all those factors in mind so it could cope with the changes that could affect the environment; otherwise, it may fail through the seasons.

The aeroplane could be affected by wind, thunder, snow, or other factors, which should be factored into the build to make it successful.

The ship can travel on water, sailing smoothly but does experience tough times as well. The vessel can only comfortably withstand regular changes because of the design.

It could be frustrating to be in the wrong environment, but in some cases, many are frustrated in the right environment. Again, it could be because of the need to understand the factors that affect the environment.

Plants have died on land, and fishes killed in the water. It is also true that many people have failed even in the right place. It could be because of the need for more awareness of the impact of environmental factors that affect their environment. Therefore, the product that will succeed must consider the relevant factor that affects the environment.

Car manufacturers do many tests to ensure that their products can withstand the challenging factors peculiar to their environment. As a result, they are confident and provide a warranty or guarantee to help the buyer rest assured that it is safe to use. The type of guarantee or warranty a manufacturer gives reflects their confidence in their products when used in the right environment. When you see reliable products, they have undergone tests in all possible harsh conditions they may go through in their environment before making them available for sale. It is not an empty promise but one made out of proven conviction. I have found that products with reliable labels have gone through a purposeful building process for the harsh environmental conditions.

When you understand the environment in which anything can flourish because you know the characteristics built into it, you can easily guarantee the product's longevity or success.

Some time ago, my wife bought some cooking utensils for the family, and I was amazed by the manufacturers' trust in the products. They came with a twenty-five years warranty. In other words, if you are using it correctly, they are sure that nothing will happen to it in 25 years. I got interested because I knew that for any manufacturer to offer—not 1 or 2 or 3 or 5, but 25 years of warranty, they must have tested it in the worst possible conditions they may face in the right environment and found that it did not fail. It is a significant risk otherwise.

We have used those products for many years under various conditions, but they still retain their characteristics. Of course, I could not prove them wrong, but I have found that the products were ready for the most unpleasant things that could happen in the right environment. They were not just good-looking but functional and retained their characteristics in their environment.

You should know that you have the features to thrive in the right environment. You are guaranteed to succeed because you can face the challenges there—they are within your ability. In addition, you can handle the challenge that may come your way.

On the other hand, the problem with the wrong environment is that the opportunity to survive may be limited. It is like doomed for failure from the start. A fish can live in water and cope with the challenges of the environment. It will search for food, run away from predators, detect the changes in temperature and move accordingly for safety, spot the signs of danger and run for safety, or listen for sounds of threat and hide. It has to do all that in the right environment to stay alive but imagine you take it out of the water and leave it on land. Even if all the food is surrounding it, without any predator running after it, carefully protected to the highest degree possible, do you think it stands a chance to survive? It will die without any predator, in the presence of food and protection, and in the company of all well-meaning well-wishers and good-thinking people. Why? It is because of the wrong environment.

Many people count the wrong factors when they fail but need to realise, just like the fish mentioned earlier, that they depend only on being in the right environment. The food will be useless to the fish on land; the protection will be worthless; the presence or lack of predators or enemies will not even matter—the wrong environment brings about the end of life. Many people have failed with many significant factors that have enabled them to succeed, like support, encouragement, nourishment, motivation, knowledge, protection, funding, sponsorship, or mentorship. Still, it has not yielded any results because of the wrong environment, which is a critical determinant.

Education has transformed many people's lives because they found something relevant to them that they could pursue, which yielded fruits of success. However, it is also true that the wrong education or knowledge has destroyed many lives. It neither benefited them nor anyone around them nor produced any valuable fruit.

Many have done more in the wrong place and have yet to see a result, while others have done less in the right place and achieved excellent results with a sense of fulfilment. The effort is great, but the area is critical. If you consider the challenges of the right place as harsh, the wrong place would even be more difficult because you may not even be able to breathe or start. These factors can help the fish when it is in water, not out of it. It may be harsh in water, but that represents the best opportunity for the fish to thrive. It only needs help to manage the challenges in that environment to flourish and grow.

It is not the challenges that make people fail, but the lack of knowledge of their existence and the unpreparedness to handle such situations contribute to their failure. They are part of the environment, and it is the nature of the place. It is possible that they will come, and one should be aware and prepared to handle them even when you are in the right place. The challenges are a reality, but understanding how to navigate the hurdles will enhance the success achieved.

The changing conditions are a constant feature of any environment, but understanding and navigating through them is crucial to succeeding. The fish cannot swim on land to avoid the challenges of the water, nor can a goat find a habitat in water to prevent the obstacles on the ground. They all have to face the challenges of their habitat and also enjoy the benefits it provides.

It is not the environment of the product that may need a change but the ability of the product to adapt to the changes. Some things should not change, even when attempting further developments and innovations, but some should; knowing the difference and making the right decision can prolong the life and success enjoyed. Therefore, You will not want to change the constant or keep the variable constant to make enduring improvements.

The right environment also comes with challenging times.

CHAPTER 12

The Design

There are some things you cannot change, but there are many things you can change that will help you become a better person and influence others. Your environment could be anything around you. It could be anywhere in the world or close to your immediate surroundings, including yourself. It could be people, laws, items, behaviours, lifestyles, policies, principles, values, and norms, amongst others. They have the same effect and can produce enhancement or diminution to anyone in that environment, just like the effect on the plants I described previously in this book.

Many people focus on themselves; only little focus is on the environment. Yet, those that impact the environment with their choices affect not only themselves but everyone who comes in contact with that environment.

You know that living in a place where there is no law or order affects everyone living there. Yes, it will impact everyone living there. For example, some people may need a better night's sleep or quietness to study well or focus. They may feel unsafe walking around or confident to allow children to play in the neighbourhood. There could be afraid of losing treasures to thieves, getting hurt, or being seen as part of evil people.

Some good folks might be in the same area, but the environment will impact their goodness. If there is a solution to the environmental issues to bring about the consciousness of law and order, it would affect every and help increase productivity.

So many people are performing below their potential because of the environment they have found themselves. So many people struggling to achieve have put in more effort than those who succeeded but could have a significant factor working against them- the power of the environment. That is why some people do less to get more results where there is law, order, and favourable infrastructure compared to a place where they are not available. Some take the pain to choose and design their environment and have found that the investment is worth the pain.

If you want to study for an examination, you will like quiet. If your environment does not provide that, it will affect your performance, and you will probably fail or underperform. You are not a failure, but your surroundings did not help release the best in you. It will affect your speed and output if you cannot focus because of family issues, domestic problems, and distractions. Your circumstances can impact your result if you do not make a deliberate effort to work on them. The same goes for anything you have the power to change around you that is affecting your potential.

The solution differs from person to person, but you can change what is around you to help increase your productivity.

It could be yourself that is serving as your distraction, making unhelpful choices affecting your goal. It could be your character, way of life, or attitude. You always want to be like the people around you, but they are not helping you. So you have chosen to keep up regardless but have yet to realise the impact on your progress.

A willing student surrounded by students with nonchalant attitudes toward education may feel demoralised. He may be affected and fall under the pressure to join, altering his desired outcome. Corruption from environmental influence has robbed many people of significance and a great future.

A young man who wants to save or invest may find it more challenging if he has friends or colleagues who spend so much on expensive lunches or parties. He would not fulfil his goal if he conforms and stays in the click. He would only remember he had such ambition but would never have enough to accomplish it because environmental forces robbed him of his future.

A young girl that desires to focus on her goal or career may suffer from environmental influence. If she only has girls that indulge in illicit and immoral activities around her, she might be drawn by the pressure and get hooked, becoming actively part of the group. The decision could absolve her to a continuous routine that offers temporary pleasure or gain but draws her away from her goal, leading to irreparable damage. The same could be the case if she is exposed to or have unguided access to men that could take advantage of her innocence. It is like a flowering plant exposed to pests; the chances of abuse or being defiled are high. It would only be a matter of time before the corruption becomes evident. Some have been victims of assault, teenage pregnancies, rape, or even death because of their environment.

They often get lured from safety to a place where no one has their best interest. As a result, they tend to move them away from their safe zones to hurt them. The farmers are wise; they usually plant seeds in nurseries in the first instance to allow them to grow under control before exposing them to harsher conditions. It helps them to thrive as they become more robust and have better chances to withstand challenges. But, again, it is about envisaging the environmental impact.

It is often true that the type of people around you can determine who will come to appreciate you or who will come to hurt you. A father or a father figure provides an environment of security for any lady. It is like a civilian in an army barracks walking around with a load of treasures. It would be hard for a thief to think of robbery in that environment.

People who desire to lose weight might find it more challenging if surrounded by people who eat a lot or buy unhealthy food.

It could be the same if the individual also stocks up on unhealthy food. When he is hungry, he only provides himself with what is against his goal as an option. He will always struggle because it is there, so instead of losing weight, he gains more because his environment has influenced him. If he desires to lose weight, he should fill his fridge and cupboards with food and snacks to help him achieve that goal. It is simple but powerful.

People who struggle to eat healthy may have created some problems by buying unhealthy foods because they are on promotion and promising to eat a little. It is punishment to surround yourself with what you do not want and then decide you will not touch it. It may be easier to surround yourself with what you know will help you, and then whenever you are hungry, you visit the fridge or store to get them. If the refrigerator only contains healthy food, guess what? That is what you would eat.

Many people have plans and resolutions that have not worked for many years because they only had a plan but never considered the influence of their environment, so they thought it would never work. For example, a man who wants to quit smoking but constantly finds himself with those who do will always get invitations and free cigarettes. If he decides to resist one or two times as long as he is in the environment, it is just a matter of time before he gets back. The solution is to find a setting that matches his desires.

No matter how much you love to drink alcohol, you cannot get drunk if you do not have one around you. If you do not want to get drunk, then do not get it or go to places that provide them. Desires could be good, but not many could withstand the influence of the environment. Many have tried only to discover that the surrounding force overcame them. They were operating in an atmosphere designed for them to fail.

The experience could be positive or negative, but if it is that powerful, why not use it to your advantage? It would be like a slide you get on; then it slides you to your goal. All you need to do is get on it or set the environment and gradually slide to the destination.

You have the power to choose, you are the architect, and you can design it as you please. Remove the negative and add the positive. You can always change to what you desire.

Some have seen the benefits of regular exercise and a healthy diet, so they built everyday practices into their routine. Some have relocated to the countryside, closer to nature, or around mountains where regular exercise is not avoidable in daily living. They also have easy access to organic or naturally grown food by default. Getting something else—unhealthy foods outside their immediate surroundings would be more challenging, which is helpful for their goal.

You can guarantee a daily exercise of walking if you have to take a bus to work and walk to and from the bus station. It is because you have already designed something that can help you by doing so. You do not need to think of exercise; as long as you have to go to work, the activity becomes fulfilled daily, even if you do not want to. It is simple! You have built it into your routine, and your environment will help you succeed. For example, a boy that takes up a paper delivery job that involves cycling every morning for one hour only needs to be motivated to go for the job; the exercise is part of and built into it. He will achieve a regular daily routine and fitness as he makes money.

People who value family life have built a structure that helps their families thrive. It could be a system that brings the parents and children together daily or as often as possible as each one fulfils their goals and roles as they grow together. The family environment then becomes an intentional design to benefit each family member.

You can build an environment that will make you flourish and helps you succeed with little or no effort. If you need focus and quietness to achieve your goal, you can build conditions that will help you achieve your goal. Determine to make choices that can help you. For example, you may need to let go of some unhelpful friends and get new ones. You may need to set out some time where you deny yourself access to some devices, relocate to a place that can help your dreams, or take advantage of quiet times by going against the tides, reading when most people sleep or getting your job done when the most people go out. You can find something that works for you and create a design that can help you.

You could get the right people around you. The people that can help you succeed. If you are a student, studying with intelligent students could motivate you and help you improve; sharing thoughts and ideas could make you better; even if you do not become as good as them, you would be better than you were. The same applies to any endeavour. For example, you would get better in the business if you had successful business people around you to guide and instruct you. It is infectious—the power of the environment. Some people have succeeded just by being in the company of successful people in the same field. You learn, share, get counsel, corrections, and assistance, and thrive. If you stay with the best, you will be better; if you stay with the better, you will be good. The environment helps you, so pay attention to where you decide to stay.

Check your environment if you keep getting into relationships that hurt or rob you. Be deliberate and surround yourself with people that share the same values, have the same worldview, share the same principles, and have the same goal or beliefs. If you are not intentional, you will have the default option, which could mean being surrounded by people of all kinds, some to hurt, harm, or take advantage of you.

There are different stages in life where you need to make significant decisions; you have a better chance when surrounded by people who can counsel and help you navigate those unique phases of your life. Unfortunately, some have failed because they did not have anyone to guide them in those critical stages of life.

The media is a powerful tool, but it can help as well as damage. You can modify your subscriptions to align with your goals. Do not allow the media to create your environment, but you can design what will help you flourish. They influence your actions and determine how you go. The media is an instrument that shapes lives and perceptions. Some have been groomed through the media to become terrorists. They only kept watching, and their desires naturally grew in such an environment as they kept giving more of the same kind to feed and keep you there. Some have developed anger, aggression, and hatred through media. Many have become rapists, womanisers, drug addicts, and killers. Some have even harmed themselves by committing suicide because of the influence of the environment. You can choose what you watch, it is a great tool, and you can design your environment to help you succeed instead of self-destructing. Many have taken advantage of media to succeed in business, relationships, marriage, education, and other areas of life. The environment can propel you to do more but ensure you have chosen the right environment.

If you deliberately surround yourself with people that do not believe in you or constantly frustrate or despise you, then it should not surprise you that you are depressed or struggle to progress. It is because you have settled in an environment that will not allow your potential to thrive.

You can design an environment that will help fulfil your goals. You can decide to quit the old unfavourable place for the new. It is your choice.

◆◆◆◆❖◆◆◆◆

You can build an environment that will make you flourish.

◆◆◆◆❖◆◆◆◆

CHAPTER 13

The Products

Every product needs an environment to flourish. You may have wondered why some products do well for a long time. One of the secrets is a favourable environment.

People buy rain boots, umbrellas, and raincoats when it is rainy. The reason they need the items is because of rain. If there is no rain, it will no longer be necessary. People buy sun cream, sunshades, and light clothing during summer because of the heat. The product's success is because of the need created by the climate. It will succeed because the environment favours it.

You might have seen some people selling ice cream, ice lolly, and cold lemonade on a beach on a sunny afternoon. You may even notice many are desperate to pay for one or more. They will patiently stand in queues to get one, so the product is popular because of the environment.

Let us consider someone selling ice packs or cold water in winter. Do you think he would get anyone interested in the product? But, on the other hand, he might need to see more people walking around because of the freezing temperatures. The failure of the product is a function of the environment. The product is good; nothing wrong with it, but which conditions are the precursor to its prosperity that the individual ignored? The influence of the environmental temperatures was not part of the thought and hence the failure of the product.

The environment must be favourable for a product to succeed or fulfil its goal. There is no wrong product, as it were; it is probably the failure to identify the appropriate environment that affects it.

Some people are interested in all kinds of things. For example, you may think a car is a write-off or damaged in an accident; some are waiting for such vehicles because they are willing to take it apart and use it for spares or repair. If you think because it got damaged in an accident, it is not valuable to anyone. You will find that some people are waiting for such; they can melt the metal to reuse for producing new cars. What you have is good if only you know where it is relevant or needed.

I have observed that when I visit a mechanic shop, there are usually shops around that sell car parts. In the same way, you will find stores that sell school supplies close to a school or corner store in a residential area that sell groceries. It is the environment for their products.

Big or super stores usually organise the items that often go together in the same aisle, shelf, or floor. It is crucial because people looking for it will search where they expect it to be.

You will do well to take football match tickets to a football club or a music concert to a music academy. Students in university would be interested in books, materials, or opportunities related to their studies; you would have found a place when you locate those that need what you have to offer.

It would be challenging to achieve much when the environment is an apparent mismatch. For example, imagine baby products sold in an older people's home or girls' hygiene products in a boys' school. What do you think of boys' wear in a girls' school? What is the sales forecast for helicopter parts in an automobile company? Or medical equipment in a law school? Something needs to be simply right. The product is brilliant, but the people that need them are elsewhere. However, you will have done a great job taking them to where you can find the people.

You may have found or observed this to be true. For example, there are cheap and costly cars, but they are in different places.

Likewise, the expensive clothing brands and budget ones are in separate locations—the people patronising the stores differ. However, each category of people knows where to go to find what they need. Therefore, everyone is willing and satisfied to pay for what they see in their appropriate environment.

Everybody needs food, and many people are happy to visit the restaurant as part of their daily routine. However, there are various types of restaurants that provide food but in different ways. For example, fast food restaurants give you food almost instantly, so you will find that the people visiting such places need something quick. On the other hand, the drive-through restaurant provides food while sitting in your car driving through the restaurant. The people visiting such locations are on the go, so they need something quick to consume on the go. Some other restaurants provide a different service where you can celebrate, have a day out, or have a family dinner. You would not go there when you are in a hurry because you have to wait and relax. They will take time to give you an experience through each process. It also means that you could be there for one or two hours having dinner, but it attracts those that want the experience they offer.

There are very few things that you may find that someone else has yet to attempt somehow, but there are opportunities to change the place to attract your unique company. Your product may be a solution that some people need, but you may need to change the environment to make a difference. You may find that success will smile at you by doing the same thing but in a different way or place.

Do you know the problem you want to solve and the place of attraction?

There is a need in every area of life and every class of society; you only need to understand the problem your product is trying to solve and the details of the environment it should attract. I hope you find the right product and the right place.

◆◆◆◆❖◆◆◆◆

You may find that success will smile at you by doing the same thing but in a different way or place.

◆◆◆◆❖◆◆◆◆

CHAPTER 14

The Change

Do you know the life process of frogs and the different stages of their development?

The lifecycle of a frog and its environment presents some engaging and fascinating lessons.

A female adult frog lays clumps of eggs in the ponds, and three weeks afterwards, tadpoles or baby frogs begin to emerge. The tailed juveniles are fully aquatic and have gills that they use for breathing. One exciting thing about tadpoles is that they cannot go on the land like mature frogs; they can only stay in water at this stage. Nevertheless, they have similarities with a fish, which makes it tricky as one can easily mistake the tadpole for a fish, especially among children or people unfamiliar with their differences.

I could recollect little children's experiences playing around freshwater or ponds. I observed as they were fascinated by the little fish-like creature in the water. They decided to take some home as they looked like fish with similar features, but they never knew the difference at the time. They were excited that the little creatures would grow up to become fishes; at least, that was their expectation, but they were wrong. It was only a matter of time before their disappointment emerged. They got what they did not bargain for and saw what they did not expect—the experience was phenomenal.

It took them some weeks to realise they had a different creature; even though it was born in water, it swam and looked like a fish, but something did not entirely agree with their thoughts as the days passed and the creature developed. The looks did not agree with expectations, and it could move out of the water and stay on land without any issues like struggling to breathe. It was not a fish but was in the environment for a period. It could take up to 14 weeks before they become frogs that could move to land and live there.[1] It was an experience of great significance.

The frustration of many is similar to those young children assuming that everything that looks like a fish or swims in water is a fish or will soon become a full-grown fish with time. It is not the water or time that will make them, but they already have the characteristics inbuilt to determine what they can potentially become.

They are only fully aquatic for a period then they move to a different environment. It is so interesting to know that where you find yourself sometimes is not a permanent place, you may only be there for a reason for a short period, and you may need to move at some point to progress and develop to maturity.

You cannot become a fish because you were born in the water. No, the water or environment can only help nourish and maximise what you already have, not what you do not have as potential. The toad is born in water as a toad that requires water for a while. So you cannot compare yourself with others even if you are all in the same place because your potential may require a change very soon.

One of the challenging things for any individual is moving to a new place. However, it could be exceptionally tough if such a person enjoyed so much comfort, had everything they needed, and so much loved the location and everything around. But, on the other hand, moving away from where you get resentment, frustration and discomfort is often an easy decision—ready to move at the slightest invitation or opportunity.

It explains why people are usually willing to remain in the same place; unfortunately, for some people, the decision to stay longer than necessary is the reason for their frustration and lack of growth.

The life cycle of an individual may involve different locations at different stages of life. Some people need help understanding that they are going through problems or challenges because they have overstayed in a particular place. You may have enjoyed it so much and grown significantly, but to progress or expand, you must leave the area.

Sometimes you have to leave not because things are bad but because your needs have changed, and you need to move to another environment suitable for your next stage of life.

The nursery of a plant is a temporary place for the plant. A time comes when it leaves the nursery because it cannot accommodate its full potential. For example, it could be a small pot with an apple seed. However, it can only stay there for a short time because the place needs to be more significant to host the future of an apple tree. It is suitable to be there at that stage, but it would cause problems except it gets moved at the right time.

Change is often tricky; hence many would not consider it, but those that do it willingly usually move ahead. On the other hand, situations or circumstances force some people to act, so you see them change when there is a crisis—when they are hurt or begin to experience losses. So a dangerous place is not often one that starts as harmful, but it could be a good place where you have overstayed your time.

Do you know where you should be at this stage of life?

You may need to leave your area to progress in your career because where you are may not be compatible with the next step. You may need some new friends to help you in your next step, which means you need to connect to such opportunities and leave some of your friends heading in a different direction.

You may know people that have left their jobs to pursue the next stage of life, starting or doing something new that became significant. Imagine if they did not know when to go, they would still be where they were or have been forced out sometime later with little or no options. Therefore, it is better to initiate the change for progress because if you knew when and where to go, you would have made a significant decision for the better.

The change could be anything anytime, but it is not a sentimental or uninformed decision. It is one that you must make intentionally based on facts. It may mean you are away from some places and be more frequently available in others to move closer to your goal. On the other hand, you may need to move out of some opportunities you once enjoyed because your new stage of life cannot manifest while you are in that old place. If you stay longer than necessary, you may see resentment, distraction, bitterness, not support, frustration, envy, confusion, and emotional manipulations that will not let you move forward.

You may have to operate in a place temporarily, just like the toad in the water, but you must recognise the time to leave and progress. So many people may mistake you for where you are, but you are still on a journey.

A time is coming when you will have developed enough to move out to progress your journey. It may be difficult for people to recognise you or your potential because of where you are. It still needs to be clarified, but a time will come when you can move to maximise your potential without any hindrance or arguments.

There is a place for you at every stage of life, do not trade it for comfort, pity, or sentiments. It would be best if you changed at the right time to experience the transformations you desire to see in your next stage of life. Then, you can find where you belong and move to where you can thrive at each phase of your life.

◆◆◆◆❖◆◆◆◆

Sometimes you have to leave not because things are bad but because your needs have changed, and you need to move to another environment suitable for your next stage of life.

◆◆◆◆❖◆◆◆◆

CHAPTER 15

The Imitation

One of the dangers of choice is the opportunity to crave something different. You have the power to choose and change, but the option or the change could become a disaster. So many people have wilfully made choices that will destroy them and their potential, some do not even realise this, and they keep hoping for things to change.

Many people often compare environments but not the characteristics of the things there. For example, the grass may seem greener on the other side, and they make a move or desire to go over only to discover that on that side. However, the grass is greener; they are not real, not living, making progress, and facing real challenges—only cosmetic values. It describes the motivation that drives some people to want to be like others or be where others are because it looks better or more colourful. One thing to note, however, is that it is not natural grass. It only seems like it, but it is not it. It is plastic that animals that feed on grass cannot eat, so every herbivorous animal that walks past will be disappointed. It is not living, so there is no natural growth or response to the environment or environmental conditions. Some people live inauthentic lives; they appear to be doing well, but they are not growing because it is deceit or cover-up; it is not real. Many people copy them and struggle to be like them but never realise it is not reality. They lure many to chase unrealistic expectations, and eventually, some may give up living because they think they are not good enough or become upset when they find the truth.

You may have found a tiger in the stores. The soft toy but the environment exposes its inauthenticity. Some people may get scared, especially when strategically placed, but they will be upset to discover they were afraid of a soft toy. The reality is that it cannot manifest like a tiger.

You will notice they can stay anywhere. You can hang them up in the air, immerse them in water, or take them to the mountaintop; it will remain the same, with no reaction or objection. But, of course, it is only possible if it is not real. If you find anything that looks like a fish out of the water and does not change, a closer examination will reveal it is probably a toy. It is unrealistic to expect a mouse to stand side by side with cheese without any reaction, except it is not real. Likewise, it is self-deceit to expect a horse to stay in a place without eating, drinking, or passing waste. It is only possible to have such if it were a toy horse. You should not need help to recognise and appreciate that it is not a real horse and hence an unrealistic outcome. Every product requires consistency in its characteristics and environment to be authentic.

More often than not, there is so much effort to make things look like something else but not function like them. They always want it to look better and present a better cosmetic outlook, but they fail to function.

It is like the perfect-looking fruits in the fruit bowl, spotless and well-rounded, but you need to get close to it to discover that they are not real. They did not grow; they cannot grow, so they can only offer cosmetic value. You cannot eat it or give it to anyone to satisfy their hunger. They are not a product of the environment they desire to settle in. They will not get the appropriate nourishment and cannot function or develop because it does not have the characteristic to support their growth and development. You may understand the anger of anyone that mistakes them for natural fruit and decides to walk away upon discovery. He would be frustrated to discover that the fruits were only plastic. An apple fruit will not just emerge from nowhere or appear anywhere. It must have a connection to an apple tree that receives resources from the soil and an environment that functions to provide for its needs.

If you only want the cosmetic value, you can change to an environment that makes you look good without any functional impact. It is like the successes that are not real, a situation where everyone thinks you are successful because of looks, but in reality, it is just a well-decorated plastic. You are only enjoying the glory of what people think you are, but you are not; you are just an imitation of it.

The fruit looks so much like an apple, but it is not. It is fake. It can only be mistaken for a fruit until the truth gets discovered. The problem is that it may be compared to the natural fruit and mistaken to be even better because it will retain the plastic look anywhere you keep it for longer.

When we try to hide from the reality of our environment, we seek a seemingly better place that will not make us better but destroy our potential. The bird can fly and look fabulous, but a mouse that attempts the same is already doomed to fail. An inbuilt characteristic enabled the birds to flourish in that environment.

Your friend may be doing well in a particular profession, but that does not mean it is a place for you. Instead, he may have some unique characteristics that allowed him to flourish there.

You may find that some people pretend to be what they are not, they spend so much to make everything artificial and challenge-free, but you will soon discover that you cannot replicate the process. It is easy for them, but everyone else finds it problematic. It only shows that something is not quite right. Every genuine product thrives in its environment and under the same expected conditions.

CHAPTER 16

The Phases

Everyone faces a strong temptation at one point or another, especially when choosing to stay or leave a place. It is not always easy, as many are yet to make informed decisions because they need to understand an environment's concept of phases and seasons.

Understanding the environment and the different phases of interaction with it is reasonable. I remember that story of a boy that got a bean seed from his mother to plant. His mother wanted to help him understand the development process through practical experience. The young boy got the bean seed, planted it in the soil, and watered it. Every necessary condition for the seed to grow was present, but the boy kept going to the ground to remove it, to check whether it had germinated. He did the same thing again on the second day; after checking, he hid the seed in the soil and continued to water it. Yet, early on the third day, he was there to see the progress, dug the ground, took the seed, had a good look, and hid it again. He said it was not growing, but he would check again later. He kept removing the seed from the soil and putting it back, but after several days he was frustrated and went to his mother. The complaint was that what she told him was invalid because the seed did not grow, and perhaps that is not the proper process, or it is not possible.

Knowing what he had done, the mother sat him down to explain that the seed had to remain in the soil—hidden, covered, alone, and undisturbed. Then, a process kicks in that will cause it to germinate. You do not have to do anything; it does it by itself. It absorbs moisture, swells, and splits open to allow growth. The root comes out first and grows into the soil downwards, attaching it firmly to the ground, creating an avenue to absorb water and nutrient from the earth. The shoot then begins to grow upward towards the sunlight and break through the soil by itself, and the fresh leaves of the new plant emerge above the ground. You only had to wait to see the plant appear; it would show up by itself, the mother informed the young boy. Furthermore, she added that the plants would also produce fruits that can benefit people with the help of all necessary factors.

There are so many lessons in the story that applies to our life. Some people need help understanding the growth phases; just like the young boy, they keep doing what is unnecessary, eventually destroying their precious work. The seed must remain covered. It is already responding to the environment—something is going on, even though you cannot see it. It is a peculiar and crucial phase; it can only do well by going through the process in hiding. You may find that many interrupt their progress because of a lack of patience. As a result, they are busy with activities when they should be waiting and waiting when they should be busy.

It is vital to understand when to act and when to give your hard work time to manifest. It is not overnight; something is happening in secret, and no one will applaud you at this phase but do not get tempted to bring your work to the open. It would be too early; wait, your work will announce itself. Leave it covered in the earth; it is going through a process and will soon appear with newness. Many keep terminating their dreams because they always get out too early, seeking fame and recognition but needing more foundation and roots to bear the weight. Be happy and satisfied to be in the secret bearing root downwards, establishing a foundation and an avenue to attach yourself to the nourishment and the stability you need before you show up. If you appear before your time, you will disappear before you shine.

It is only a phase; it is only for a while, and when the time comes, you will emerge with a strong foundation. For example, a seed stays covered in the soil for a period, germinating and taking root in the downward direction before you can see the stem in the upward movement and fruits on the plant.

Many people want to refrain from labouring quietly and in secret. A stage of life where you would be alone, not being known, seen or acknowledged. A time of life that seems you are going down—ignored, left behind, wasting away, and alone. It is a stage and a phase similar to the foundation of a building; the foundation goes down first before you can see a skyscraper that will go upward. You may need to sacrifice, deny yourself, die to selfishness, and allow something new to break forth. If you can maximise the time in the secret by investing productively in a great future, you will emerge with a structure standing on a solid base.

The environment may be correct, but if the activities are wrong, the outcome could be frustration. Therefore, it is crucial to know what you should do at the different phases of development, even in the right environment. For example, some people have put in so much hard work to build a future they have done the right thing, but impatience or comparing themselves with others made them ignore or neglect their assignment to find a new place. They are like the little boy expecting the seed in a matter of hours, and when it is not showing up, they remove it or forget about it to try something popular and fashionable.

Some trees have grown and produced fruits, but the person who planted the seed forgot about it when he did not see anything immediately. There are so many trees producing fruits for other people, but those that grew them are still wandering around asking for help because they did not even believe in their seed—they gave up and forgot about it. What you are doing may not become great today, but if you persist, another phase will come, and it will become a mighty tree, producing fruits.

Many people that became great have endured the challenges of the right environment. They invested time to build processes and programs that took time to mature, but they were patient and reaped the continuous dividends many years after without the need to keep repeating the same labour. Of course, sometimes they fail, but they stay there. It seems all is going bad; just like the seed, it rots, but a new life emerges after some time. It is not the final result; it is only part of the process.

There are four common weather seasons, and not all are pleasant to one's feelings. For example, summer and winter are not the same; neither are spring and fall. They present different challenges or advantages, but they keep it within that season, so you can rest assured that it will soon pass. You do not have to forgo your labour and investment because of a transient change. There are temporary changes at different times, like wind, storm, cold, heat, or rain, but they should not scare you from your future. It is a phase or a season and will soon pass away.

The apple seed grows to become a tree, and every year it faces different seasons, but it still stands, producing fruit in its seasons. So it is encouraging to know that the seasons are temporary and we can stay put till our victory emerges.

There is a season the farmland looks clean because the seeds in the soil are going through a process. Some time afterwards, another season comes when you see the leaves, and another season comes when the fruits emerge, getting ripe for the season for harvest. You cannot expect harvest in the planting season, nor can you expect planting season during harvest. You must understand the seasons and the one you are in and act accordingly to get the best result.

You will find that in one location, it is winter, and in the same place, you will still experience summer if you are patient. You cannot change the season, but you can make the most of the seasons to fulfil your goal.

A challenging time does not mean the seed is terrible or the environment needs fixing. It could mean a phase that is necessary for growth and development. It is only a season that will soon give way to the next season; it is automatic. You cannot do anything to change the season, but you can do all you can to adapt and make the most of every season. It would help to understand life's phases, especially the ones you find yourself in at one point or another. It may be better than you think. You may not need to do anything; you may only need to wait for the time to pass. I hope you understand the phases and seasons of life and act wisely to secure a great future.

◆◆◆◆❖◆◆◆◆

A challenging time does not mean the seed is terrible or the environment needs fixing. It could mean a phase that is necessary for growth and development.

◆◆◆◆❖◆◆◆◆

CHAPTER 17

The Potential

Many great things happen because greatness is inbuilt, yes, it is in everyone, but they take advantage of the appropriate environment to realise the potential already there. The environment will not develop what you do not have. It only enhances, empowers, and grows what is already available. A little in the right environment can become tremendous and massive if the potentials meet with the relevant resources in the environment.

The mustard is a tiny seed of about 1 to 2 millimetres in diameter. It is about 9 to 19 times bigger than a penny, with a diameter of approximately 19.05 millimetres.[1] It is so tiny and looks insignificant when you see the seed. However, it is full of potential that can only find expression in the right environment.

If you plant the seed in the soil with other favourable environmental factors, you gradually begin to see the transformation. It releases the abilities within, and a new plant emerges and grows under advantageous conditions. You will find that in ideal situations, some species can grow up to 30 feet tall and the width much as their height. It is an embodiment of value, with the fruits, seeds, branches, and the tree itself providing benefits for animals and plants.

Remember, this a tiny seed that you may decide to ignore by leaving it on the table where the abilities will not find expression or maximise their potential. However, the same can benefit several people because someone decided to take the responsibility to research the right environment conducive to its potential to flourish.

So many people are yet to yield the value they carry because they are in the wrong place. The potential is still there, but there is nothing to trigger them. There is nothing to activate the seed to begin to sprout to develop into a tree that will yield fruits, representing value to their generation.

Many spend their life looking for what they already have to make better, a place where they should not be in the first place. However, the story will differ if they seek a place to release what they have within them. They may soon discover the greatness inbuilt, which needs to connect to the right environment to initiate the automatic release.

One grain grows into a tree to produce a tree with fruits and seeds. When one person gets it right, he opens the way for many others to benefit from his fruits and grains. The seeds can also release the potential to produce another tree with fruits and seeds. As time progressed, more fruits and grains would become available from the first tree. It means that more can become ready for planting from all who benefited from the first tree. Furthermore, more seeds will produce more trees, fruits, and grains.

The next generation will also have the opportunity to continue the cycle. Many more people plant more seeds to produce more fruits and more grains. It will continue because it already has the inbuilt potential to do so. The only thing that will stop the continuous success is when everyone stops planting the seeds in a favourable environment.

When you have many trees with many fruits and seeds, you need to allow the inbuilt potential to do the work, yet you can add value and keep adding value every season.

You should only expect the greatness of a tree with fruits and seeds if there is first the responsibility of committing them to a favourable environment. You already have a tremendous potential inbuilt but what may be lacking is the advantageous conditions to make them prosper. Then, when you find your way to that place, the potential will leap and yield, producing trees, fruits, and seeds.

Please use the potential wisely because it will not produce anything otherwise. A seed can remain a seed for thirty years if it does not get planted. It could also experience generational transformations if it can find its way to the right place in the first year. The one seed, after thirty years, would have become many trees, fruits, and grains.

There is something in you crying for expression. There is something within you that desires to connect to the source. The seed needs to connect to the soil, the fish needs to stay in the water, and every human needs to attach to the right and original place. You need the source to unleash and maximise your potential. There is something within everyone that needs the right environment to activate the hidden treasures. It is automatic—it works in the right place. So connect and remain connected because there is something more about you that you have not yet realised. You will find fulfilment and joy if you do.

Choose to leave where you are to where you ought to be. You already have greatness in you. You only need to connect to the source to see it come to pass. I hope you release your potential to benefit your generation and many more.

References

Chapter 1: The Place

[1] San Diego Zoo Wildlife Alliance, "Camel | San Diego Zoo Animals & Plants," Sandiegozoo.org, 2019. https://animals.sandiegozoo.org/animals/camel (Accessed Jun. 11 2022).

[2] National Geographic Society, "Arabian Camels Eat Cacti With Hardened Mouth Structures," Animals, May 30, 2018. https://www.nationalgeographic.com/animals/article/camels-cactus-mouth-papillae-animals (Accessed Jun. 11 2022).

Chapter 3: The Chance

[1] B. Turner, "Baby minke whale

euthanized after getting trapped in Thames River," livescience.com, May 11, 2021. https://www.livescience.com/baby-minke-whale-put-down-london.html (accessed Jun. 11, 2022).

[2] BBC, "Withernsea: Work Begins to Remove Dead Whales from Beach," BBC News, Dec. 29, 2020. Accessed: Jun. 11, 2022. [Online]. Available: https://www.bbc.co.uk/news/uk-england-humber-55475413

Chapter 4: The Dormant

[1] Voice of America, "Israel Harvests Dates from 2,000 Year-Old Seeds," www.voanews.com, Oct. 13, 2021. https://www.voanews.com/a/israel-harvests-dates-from-2000-year-old-seeds-/6269266.html (accessed Jun. 16, 2022).

[2] Ben Anthony Horton,AFP, "Ancient seeds defy sell-by 'date' to become oldest ever germinated," euronews. Oct. 09, 2021. Accessed: Jun. 16, 2022. [Online]. Available: https://www.euronews.com/green/2021/10/09/these-2000-year-old-dates-have-been-brought-back-to-life-by-scientists

[3] V. News, "Israel Harvests Dates from 2000 Year Old Seeds," YouTube. Oct. 13, 2021. Accessed: Jun. 16, 2022. [Online]. Available: https://www.youtube.com/watch?v=dNI83UvOonc

Chapter 7: The Project

[1] Eden Project, "Mediterranean Biome," Eden Project. https://www.edenproject.com/visit/things-to-do/mediterranean-biome [Accessed Jul.

16 2022].

Chapter 8: The Function

[1] RSPCA (2019). Why Is Wallowing Important for Pig welfare? – RSPCA Knowledgebase. [online] RSPCA. Available at: https://kb.rspca.org.au/knowledge-base/why-is-wallowing-important-for-pig-welfare/. (Accessed Jul. 16 2022).

[2] wonderopolis.org. (n.d.). Why Do Pigs Like Mud? | Wonderopolis. [online] Available at: https://wonderopolis.org/wonder/why-do-pigs-like-mud. (Accessed Jul. 16 2022).

Chapter 9: The Engrafted

[1] CNN, W.M., Special to (n.d.). Growing 40 types of fruit on one tree. [online] CNN. Available at:

https://edition.cnn.com/2015/08/03/living/tree-40-fruit-sam-van-aken-feat/index.html. (Accessed Jul. 16 2022).

Chapter 11: The Constant

[1] Research Gate (2019). ResearchGate | Share and Discover Research. [online] ResearchGate. Available at: https://www.researchgate.net/publication/227938875_Foraging_behaviour_and_hunting_success_of_lions_in_Queen_Elizabeth_National_Park_Uganda. (Accessed Dec. 10 2022).

[2] Siyabona Africa (2022). Kruger National Park Lion Facts - Big Predators - Lions. [online] www.krugerpark.co.za. Available at: https://www.krugerpark.co.za/Kruger_National_Park_Wildlife-travel/kruger-park-wildlife-lions.html. (Accessed Dec. 10 2022).

Chapter 14: The Change

[1] National Geographic Kids, "The Frog Life Cycle for Kids," National Geographic Kids, Mar. 31, 2021. https://www.natgeokids.com/uk/discover/science/nature/frog-life-cycle/ (accessed Dec. 10, 2022).

Chapter 17: The Potential

[1] Gwen, "20 Mind-blowing Mustard Tree Facts That You Probably Didn't Know," TheFragrantGarden, Dec. 07, 2022. https://thefragrantgarden.com/mustard-tree-facts/ (accessed Dec. 10, 2022).

Thank you

Thank you for investing in this book. I hope you enjoyed reading it as much as it has been a pleasure for me to write it, and I trust that it has helped you.

It would be helpful to me and many others if you could share your experience by way of a review or a comment.

Please write to:

iph@TheServantandKing.com

We would be glad to hear from you.

Looking for more?

Please visit:

www.TheServantandKing.com

Automated: The concept of continuous results with diminishing involvement.

IF YOU KEEP DOING THE SAME THING
OVER AND OVER AGAIN AND EXPECTING
THE SAME RESULT: THINK AUTOMATION.

Let this book inspire you to productivity!

Available on Amazon or your local bookstore.

Essential: Finding Relevance in the Midst of Crisis

WHEN ONE DOOR CLOSES
ANOTHER DOOR OPENS; BUT WE SO OFTEN LOOK
SO LONG AND SO REGRETFULLY UPON THE CLOSED
DOOR, THAT WE DO NOT SEE THE ONES WHICH OPEN FOR US.
— ALEXANDER GRAHAM BELL

In Essential, you will find some clear and actionable advice that will help to restore hope and encourage you to step out and make the most of any situation. You are essential because you can make yourself relevant even when things change.

Available on Amazon or your local bookstore.

www.ingramcontent.com/pod-product-compliance
Lightning Source LLC
Chambersburg PA
CBHW071439090426
42737CB00011B/1714